-FOODS OF-
JAPAN

by Christine VeLure Roholt

BELLWETHER MEDIA • MINNEAPOLIS, MN

Library of Congress Cataloging-in-Publication Data

VeLure Roholt, Christine, author.
 Foods of Japan / by Christine VeLure Roholt.
    pages cm. -- (Express. Cook with Me)
 Summary: "Information accompanies step-by-step instructions on how to cook Japanese food. The
text level and subject matter are intended for students in grades 3 through 7"-- Provided by publisher.
 Audience: Age 7-12.
 Audience: Grades 3-7.
 Includes bibliographical references and index.
 ISBN 978-1-62617-120-6 (hardcover : alk. paper)
1. Cooking, Japanese--Juvenile literature. 2. Food habits--Japan--Juvenile literature. 3. Japan--Social
life and customs--Juvenile literature. I. Title.
 TX724.5.J3V45 2014
 641.5952--dc23
                          2014008462

This edition first published in 2015 by Bellwether Media, Inc.

Printed in the United States of America, North Mankato, MN.

Table of Contents

Cooking the Japanese Way

At the heart of Japanese culture is **balance**. Japanese people strive for this in many areas of life and especially at dinnertime. Many follow **Buddhist** practices to find the balance they desire. They use the number five as a guide in their search. To them, it is a **symbol** of perfect balance.

Japanese cooking engages all five senses. It also features five main colors and offers five unique flavors. Plates are colored by white, black, green, red, and yellow foods. Dishes have salty, sweet, sour, bitter, and *umami* flavors. The umami flavor tastes **savory** and is the Japanese word for "yummy." Foods are boiled, grilled, steamed, fried, or served raw. A meal often includes foods prepared using at least four of these methods.

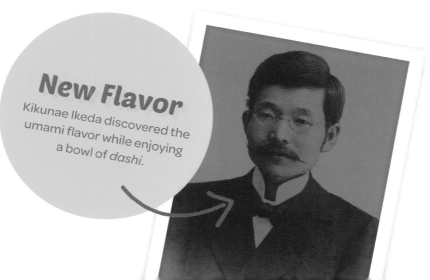

New Flavor
Kikunae Ikeda discovered the umami flavor while enjoying a bowl of *dashi*.

Eating the Japanese Way

Japanese people show appreciation for their food. Before they eat, they say, "*Itadakimasu*." This word means "I gratefully receive." Then they give thanks for a meal again after the last bite. To show respect during a meal, Japanese people have good table manners. These include using chopsticks, or *hashi*, properly. Japanese people never play with or point their chopsticks.

Lift and Sip

It is proper to lift a soup bowl and use it like a cup.

Japanese people also have special places for different foods. A rice bowl sits to the left of a soup bowl. **Pickled** vegetables and a side dish are placed behind the bowls. Chopsticks lie in front of the bowls. If noodles are served, they go in the soup's usual spot.

Regional Foods

Many regions in Japan are known for unique food dishes. These dishes are often made with local ingredients and **traditional** recipes. Some of them are popular all over Japan but prepared differently in each region.

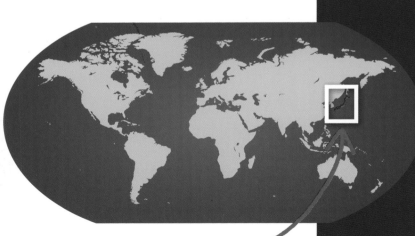

Okinawa
chanpuru:
Stir-fry with tofu, pork, and goya

Where is Japan?

Chūgoku

fugu:
Pufferfish served with the poisonous parts removed

Hokkaido

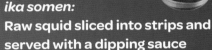

ika somen:
Raw squid sliced into strips and served with a dipping sauce

Tōhoku

wanko soba:
A serving of soba, or buckwheat, noodles in a small bowl

Kansai

yudofu:
Tofu cooked in hot water with dried seaweed

Kyushu

mizutaki:
Chicken and vegetables in a broth and served with *ponzu*

N
W   E
S

9

Tea and Treats

Green tea is the drink of choice in Japan. People drink it hot and cold throughout the day. Restaurants serve it for free with meals. *Matcha*, the powdered version, is used for a special tea ceremony called the "Way of Tea." This ceremony is both an art and a **spiritual** practice.

matcha

wagashi

The tea ceremony also features sweet treats called *wagashi*. Some wagashi are made with *mochi*, or pounded rice, and filled with sweetened bean paste. The sweets help balance the bitter taste of matcha. Daily meals in Japan often finish with fruit for dessert.

Getting Ready to Cook

Before you begin cooking, read these safety reminders. Make sure you also read the recipes you will follow. You will want to gather all the ingredients and cooking tools before you start.

Safety Reminders

 Ask an adult for permission to start cooking. An adult should be near when you use kitchen appliances or a sharp knife.

 Wash your hands with soapy water before you start cooking. Wash your hands again if you lick your fingers or handle raw meat.

 If you have long hair, tie it back. Remove any bracelets or rings that you have on.

 Wear an apron when you cook. It will protect food from dirt and your clothes from spills and splatters.

 Always use oven mitts when handling hot cookware. If you accidentally burn yourself, run the burned area under cold water and tell an adult.

 If a fire starts, call an adult immediately. Never throw water on a fire. Baking soda can smother small flames. A lid can put out a fire in a pot or pan. If flames are large and leaping, call 911 and leave the house.

 Clean up the kitchen when you are done cooking. Make sure all appliances are turned off.

Okonomiyaki

oh-KO-no-me-yah-KEY

Savory Japanese Pancake
Serves 4

Okonomiyaki is a favorite dish of many Japanese kids. It is sometimes referred to as Japanese pizza. It can be prepared with many different toppings. Popular toppers include corn, potatoes, bacon, eel, mayonnaise, and dried seaweed.

What You'll Need

- 1 3/4 cups cabbage
- 1 cup vegetables (your choice)
- 1 cup beef or pork
- 6 eggs
- 1 tablespoon milk
- 1 tablespoon corn starch
- 1/2 cup flour
- 1/3 cup tempura flakes (optional)
- 1 tablespoon vegetable oil
- 1 tablespoon dried bonito flakes (optional)
- 1 tablespoon mayonnaise
- knife
- bowl
- whisk
- frying pan
- spatula

Let's Make It!

1

Finely chop the cabbage and other vegetables, then thinly slice the meat.

2

In a bowl, mix the eggs, milk, and flour to make the batter.

3

Stir in the cabbage, vegetables, corn starch, and tempura flakes.

4

Add a tablespoon of vegetable oil to a frying pan on medium-high heat. Pour the batter into the frying pan, then lay the meat on top. Cook for about 5 minutes.

5

Use a spatula to flip the pancake. Then cook the other side.

Enjoy!

Transfer the pancake to a plate when it is fully cooked. Cover it with mayonnaise, okonomiyaki sauce, and bonito flakes.

Make the Sauce

Okonomiyaki sauce is available at many Asian markets. You can also make your own sauce at home with these ingredients:

- 6 tablespoons ketchup
- 1 tablespoon soy sauce
- 3 tablespoons Worcestershire sauce

Corn Potage

corn PO-tahj

Creamy Corn Soup
Serves 4

Almost every family-style restaurant serves corn potage in Japan. Japanese people loved this French creation so much they made their own version. Many grocery stores sell it as a powder mix.

What You'll Need

- 1/2 onion
- 1 tablespoon butter
- 1 3/4 cups corn
- 1 3/4 cups milk
- 2 bouillon cubes vegetable stock (substitute: chicken stock)
- salt
- pepper
- parsley
- knife
- large saucepan
- stick blender
- ladle

Let's Make It!

1

Finely chop the onion.

2

Melt the butter in a saucepan over medium heat, then sauté the onion for about 5 minutes or until soft.

3

Add the corn, then cook for 1 minute.

4

Add the milk and bouillon cubes, then reduce to medium-low heat.

Enjoy!

Use a stick blender to mix the soup in the saucepan, then season with salt and pepper. Ladle the soup into bowls, then add the parsley.

Easy to Find
Corn potage can be purchased from vending machines in Japan.

Temari-Zushi

tay-MAR-ee-ZOO-she

Handmade Sushi Balls
Makes 40 Balls

Temari-zushi is a colorful sushi dish of formed rice balls. Ingredients can be mixed and matched to form a variety of delicious combinations. This popular food is usually enjoyed during celebrations.

What You'll Need

- 3 cups sushi rice
- 3 1/2 cups water
- 5 tablespoons rice vinegar
- 3 tablespoons sugar
- 1 tablespoon salt
- saucepan with lid
- strainer
- spoon
- rice paddle
- plastic wrap (optional)

Suggested Toppings

- avocados
- carrots
- cucumbers
- eggs (scrambled)
- green onions
- nori seaweed
- salmon
- shrimp
- tuna

Let's Make It!

First, let's make the rice

1. Add the rice to the saucepan, then cover with water. Stir the rice, then drain the water. Repeat until the water is clear when drained.

2. Add 3 1/2 cups of water to the rice, then bring to a boil over high heat. Cover the pot with the lid, then reduce the heat to low. Cook for 20 minutes or until the water is absorbed.

3. Transfer the rice to a bowl, then let cool for 15 minutes.

1

To make the sushi vinegar, warm the rice vinegar, sugar, and salt in a saucepan over low heat. Stir until the sugar and salt dissolve.

2

When the rice is cool and sticky to the touch, spread the sushi vinegar equally over the rice.

3

Shape the rice into balls. Use water or use plastic wrap to keep the rice from sticking to your hands.

4

Add toppings to your creations, then serve cold.

Yakisoba

yah–KEY–so–BA

Japanese Fried Noodles
Serves 4

Although *yakisoba* was first cooked in China, it is now a popular dish all over Japan. It is sold by street carts and restaurants, but it is also made in the home.

What You'll Need

- 1/2 cup carrots
- 1/3 cup onions
- 1/2 cup cabbage
- 1/2 cup beef (substitute: chicken or pork)
- 20 ounces cooked ramen noodles
- 6 tablespoons yakisoba sauce (substitute: Worcestershire sauce)
- 1 tablespoon olive oil
- knife
- large frying pan
- spatula

Let's Make It!

1

Thinly slice the carrots and onions. Then chop the cabbage and cut the meat into small pieces.

2

Pour the olive oil in the frying pan and place over medium-high heat. Fry the meat until it is almost fully cooked.

3

Add the onions and carrots, then fry until they are softened.

4

Add the cabbage, then cook until it is softened.

5

Separate the cooked noodles, then stir them into the mixture.

Enjoy!

Stir in the yakisoba sauce, then stir-fry for 1–2 minutes.

Did You Know?

Yakisoba means "fried noodles" in Japanese.

Glossary

balance—an equal or proportional amount of parts or ingredients

Buddhist—related to Buddhism; Buddhism is a religion started in India that aims for enlightenment.

pickled—preserved in vinegar

savory—something that tastes salty or spicy

spiritual—of or relating to someone's personal beliefs

symbol—something that stands for something else

traditional—related to the stories, beliefs, or ways of life that families or groups hand down from one generation to another

To Learn More

AT THE LIBRARY

McCulloch, Julie. *Japan*. Chicago, Ill.: Heinemann Library, 2009.

Mofford, Juliet Haines. *Recipe and Craft Guide to Japan*. Hockessin, Del.: Mitchell Lane Publishers, 2011.

Wagner, Lisa. *Cool Chinese and Japanese Cooking: Fun and Tasty Recipes for Kids*. Minneapolis, Minn.: ABDO Pub., 2011.

ON THE WEB

Learning more about Japan is as easy as 1, 2, 3.

1. Go to www.factsurfer.com.

2. Enter "Japan" into the search box.

3. Click the "Surf" button and you will see a list of related web sites.

With factsurfer.com, finding more information is just a click away.

Index